To The Rescue
EMERGENCY VEHICLES

Genevieve Boyer

Contents

These are the places you can
see emergency vehicles:

Emergency vehicles help to keep people safe. When someone is injured, in danger or when people need help, emergency vehicles come to the rescue!

AMBULANCE

STAR OF LIFE

RA-2439

If someone's car is in an accident, breaks down or parks in the wrong spot, a **tow truck** can come along and tow the car away.

Tow Truck

Some tow trucks move cars by lifting either the front or rear wheels of the car and dragging it behind them.

Other tow trucks lift cars onto a flatbed using a winch.

Heavy duty tow trucks have more powerful engines than regular tow trucks. They have strong wheel-lift devices and winches.

Special, super-strong tow trucks tow big rigs, dump trucks, fire trucks, buses and other heavy vehicles.

Heavy Duty Tow Truck

A heavy duty tow truck can safely lift a truck heavier than itself without tipping.

An ambulance takes people who are very sick or hurt to the hospital.

Wee-ooo-wee-ooo-wee-ooo! An ambulance has a loud siren and flashing lights to tell other drivers to move out of the way.

8

Ambulance

The people who work in ambulances are called paramedics. A paramedic is trained to take care of sick or injured people until they can see a doctor at the hospital.

Inside the Ambulance

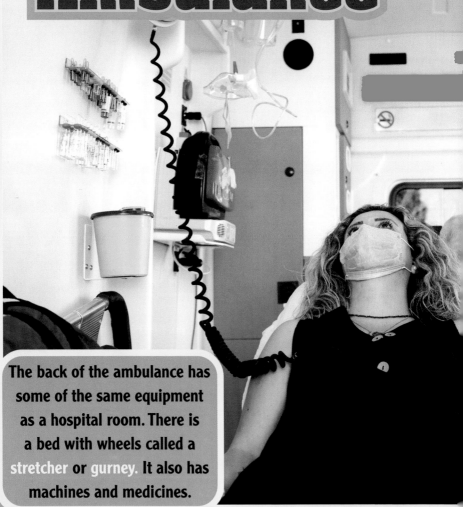

The back of the ambulance has some of the same equipment as a hospital room. There is a bed with wheels called a stretcher or gurney. It also has machines and medicines.

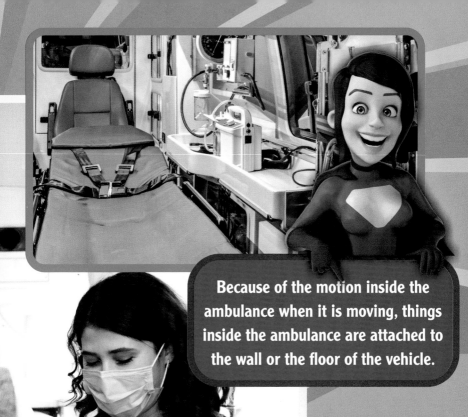

Because of the motion inside the ambulance when it is moving, things inside the ambulance are attached to the wall or the floor of the vehicle.

The paramedics use a radio to talk to other rescue workers, like 911 dispatchers, nurses and doctors at a hospital.

At some events, like parades and festivals, paramedics ride bicycle ambulances. Bicycles can go places that large ambulance vehicles cannot.

The bicycles carry first aid supplies to help injured people until an ambulance arrives.

Some bicycle ambulances are pedal bikes, and some are motorbikes.

Bicycle Ambulance

13

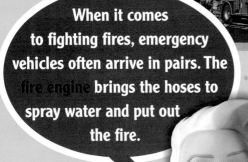

When it comes to fighting fires, emergency vehicles often arrive in pairs. The fire engine brings the hoses to spray water and put out the fire.

The fire truck brings the ladder to help firefighters rescue people from burning buildings.

Fighting Fires

The cab of a fire truck or fire engine has a radio so firefighters can talk to other emergency workers.

It is important to call 911 when there is a fire. The 911 operator can talk with the closest fire hall to get the fire fighters there quickly.

The sides of the fire engine carry equipment to help fight fires:

- hoses
- fire extinguishers
- tool kits
- air tanks
- breathing masks

Fire Engine

The fire engine also has valves that control the flow of water in the hoses.

The fire truck ladder helps firefighters get a good angle to spray water or foam **fire retardant** on the flames. Many fire truck ladders can extend to 100 feet (30 metres), about half the length of a hockey rink, or more!

Firefighters also use the ladder to rescue people trapped high up in buildings. Fire trucks carry first aid equipment to help take care of the people they rescue.

Fire trucks have floodlights to help firefighters see well in the dark.

Fire Truck

19

Airports have their own fire engines, often called **crash tenders**. They come to the rescue if there is a fire at the airport.

FIRE 5

Airport Crash Tender

An airport crash tender has a large built-in water tank, and a tank of foam fire retardant. It doesn't have a ladder, but often it has an extendable hose that looks a bit like a ladder.

The crash tenders will sometimes do a water salute to celebrate the first flight of a new type of airplane, the start of a new airline or the arrival of a famous person. A water salute usually lasts about 2 minutes and can use up to 3000 gallons (11,350 litres) of water. That is about 38 full bathtubs of water!

HAZMAT *ive* Truck

HAZMAT is short for hazardous materials. When an emergency involves dangerous chemicals, the HAZMAT truck comes to the rescue!

HAZMAT 18
RESPONSE TEAM

A HAZMAT truck safely takes care of leaking oil, gas or other dangerous liquids and powders that can catch fire easily or make people sick.

Sometimes the people who work in HAZMAT vehicles wear special suits to keep them safe from the dangerous chemicals they work with.

Fuchs are army trucks that have equipment to test for harmful chemicals, radiation and nuclear waste that can make people sick.

An infrared detector on the fuch can check for harmful chemicals in the air. A sampling station at the back of the fuch collects water or plants for testing.

24

The strong walls and windows keep the soldiers safe. The tires also collect information about dangerous chemicals on the ground as the truck drives.

Fuch Army
HAZMAT Vehicle

Police officers help keep people safe by responding to 911 calls, making sure drivers are following traffic rules and checking out suspicious activity.

Police cars take police officers where they need to go quickly!

HOUSTON POLIC

TEXAS
113•0764

Police cars have sirens that can make many different sounds. The wail sound switches slowly between high and low tones. The yelp sound switches quickly between high and low tones. Police use the yelp siren when they are in a real hurry.

26

Police Car

Some police cars look like regular cars until they turn on their lights and sirens. These cars are sometimes called ghost cars.

42061

EMERGENCY
911

HOUSTON

POLICE

NON EMERGENCY
713-884-3131

The driver's seat of a police car has a computer and a radio next to it. The radio allows police officers to talk to other emergency workers.

The back of the police car is called a cage. A metal screen or strong clear plastic divider behind the front seat protects the police officers from people in the cage.

COMM

Inside A Police Car

Did you know? Some nicknames for police cars are panda car, jam sandwich and gumball machine!

SWAT stands for Special Weapons And Tactics.

Some SWAT vehicles carry tools and weapons, such as protective clothing, guns, rifles, shields, battering rams and stun grenades.

Other SWAT vehicles are made to safely take police officers, negotiators and medics to dangerous emergencies, like bank robberies or kidnappings.

These armoured vehicles can provide protection from gunshots. They are used when special equipment or large teams of emergency workers are needed.

SWAT Vehicle

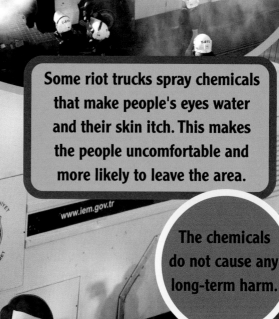

Some riot trucks spray chemicals that make people's eyes water and their skin itch. This makes the people uncomfortable and more likely to leave the area.

The chemicals do not cause any long-term harm.

Riot Vehicle

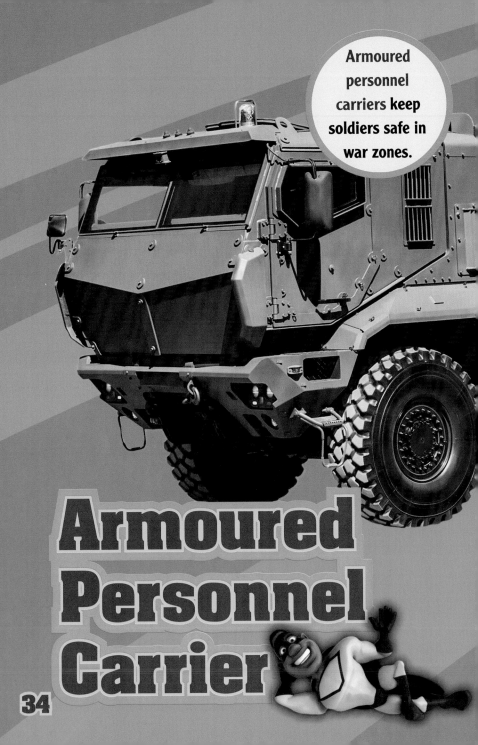

Armoured personnel carriers keep soldiers safe in war zones.

Armoured Personnel Carrier

They are usually made with steel or aluminum to protect against bullets. The windows have bulletproof glass.

In the back are seats for the soldiers and only small windows so the soldiers can see what is happening outside.

Many armoured personnel carriers are painted in a color that camouflages them in their surroundings.

Some have wheels, but others have all-terrain tracks so they can go places where there are no roads.

Other Armoured Carriers

Some armoured personnel carriers are ambulances that carry injured soldiers to the hospital.

Road-laying Truck

The road-laying truck can lay down a temporary road for other vehicles to drive on.

This army truck can lay a road over unstable ground, like mud, marsh or sand, where vehicles might otherwise get stuck.

When the army vehicles are done using the temporary road, it can be rolled or folded back up until it is needed again.

39

Bridge-laying Armoured Vehicle

A **bridge-laying armoured vehicle** can build a bridge for other vehicles to drive over. The vehicle carries the bridge to where it is needed and then puts it in place in less than two minutes. When the bridge is no longer needed the vehicle picks it up again.

This vehicle can make a bridge that is about 85 feet (26 metres) long. That is about as long as three school buses parked one in front of the other!

This bridge-laying vehicle needs three people to operate it: a driver, a commander and a bridge operator. They stay safe inside the armoured vehicle as it lays down and picks up the bridge.

41

Air Drop Rescue Vehicle

The **air drop rescue vehicle** can be dropped from an airplane or helicopter into remote areas using guided parachutes.

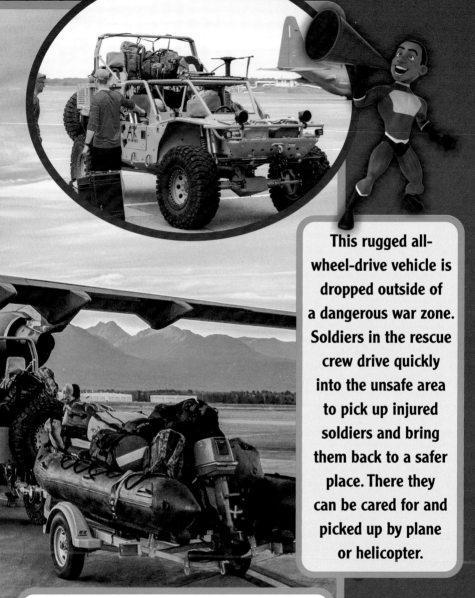

This rugged all-wheel-drive vehicle is dropped outside of a dangerous war zone. Soldiers in the rescue crew drive quickly into the unsafe area to pick up injured soldiers and bring them back to a safer place. There they can be cared for and picked up by plane or helicopter.

This air drop rescue vehicle can use many different types of fuel, like gas, diesel and jet fuel. It stays stable on steep slopes and keeps the rescue workers safe if it tips over.

43

Sometimes a ground ambulance cannot get to someone who is hurt or sick quickly enough. That is when an air ambulance comes to the rescue!

44

The medical staff in the air ambulance take care of the patient until the helicopter lands at the hospital.

An air ambulance is also used to quickly move a sick or injured person from one hospital to another.

Air Ambulance

45

Search and rescue helicopters **help get people out of places where cars and trucks cannot go.**

Search and Rescue Helicopter

If the helicopter cannot land close to the sick, injured or lost person, the rescuer can be lowered to the injured person.

The rescuer and the injured person can be lifted out of the area and carried to safety in a harness or a basket.

47

An airtanker is an airplane that carries water to a forest fire. Water scoopers fill up with water by skimming the surface of nearby lakes. Their tanks can fill up in 12 seconds!

Airtanker

The airtanker drops water over the forest fire to put out the flames. Water scoopers can carry up to 1600 gallons (6000 L) of water. That is more than 38 bathtubs full of water!

Sometimes, instead of water, an airtanker will drop fire retardant to put out the fire. Very Large Airtankers (VLATs) can carry as much as 17,500 gallons (66,245 L) of fire retardant. That is about as much as 416 full bathtubs!

Sometimes helicopters join the aircraft firefighting team.

Like the airtanker, the helitanker fills its tank with water at a nearby lake.

Helitanker

It carries the water to the fire.

Then it drops the water onto the fire.

Most helitankers carry about 350 gallons (1325 L) of water, which is more than 8 full bathtubs. The largest helitanker can carry about 3000 gallons (11,355 L) of water, which is about 71 full bathtubs.

Police Helicopter

Police helicopters work with police cars to watch what is happening on the ground. Most police helicopters can fly for two to three hours before coming back down to the ground to refuel.

POLICE

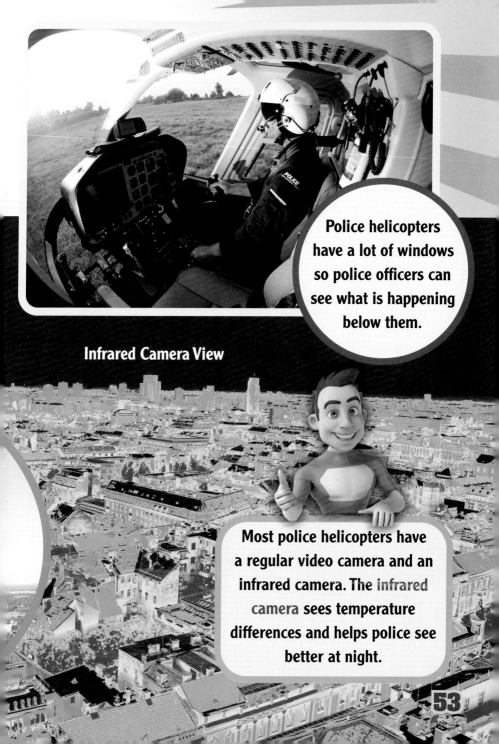

Police helicopters have a lot of windows so police officers can see what is happening below them.

Infrared Camera View

Most police helicopters have a regular video camera and an infrared camera. The infrared camera sees temperature differences and helps police see better at night.

An army transport helicopter carries soldiers to and from places they need to protect.

It usually lands on the ground so the soldiers can get out.

54

Sometimes the helicopter stays in the air, and the soldiers rappel down to the ground using special ropes.

Army Transport Helicopter

Heavy Lift Helicopter

The **CH-53 Super Stallion** helicopter can carry up to 36,000 pounds (16,330 kg), about as much as three male African elephants!

These huge helicopters can also carry boats and even other helicopters!

Super Heavy Lifting

Some heavy lift helicopters have two rotors, with two engines. Having twice as many rotors helps create more lift. It is also safer just in case one engine fails.

The supplies, cars, equipment, boats and helicopters can then help with other rescue missions!

59

Rescue Drone

When there is a natural disaster, like an earthquake or an avalanche, a drone may come to the rescue! Drones also help to find people lost in the wilderness.

The drone can play a recorded message to let the missing person know that someone is looking for them.

SERVE ON

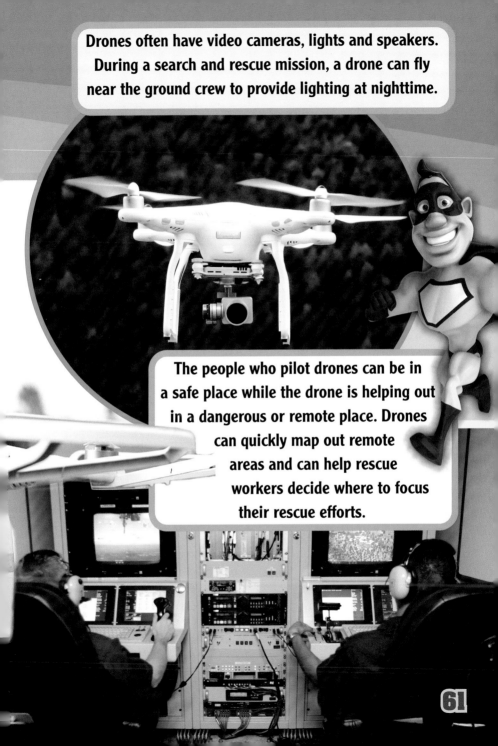

Drones often have video cameras, lights and speakers. During a search and rescue mission, a drone can fly near the ground crew to provide lighting at nighttime.

The people who pilot drones can be in a safe place while the drone is helping out in a dangerous or remote place. Drones can quickly map out remote areas and can help rescue workers decide where to focus their rescue efforts.

Sometimes the fastest way to save someone at sea is by boat. Water ambulance to the rescue!

AMBULANCE

A captain pilots the boat, and two paramedics take care of the hurt people until they can get to the hospital.

A water ambulance usually has flashing lights and sirens just like a ground ambulance.

STAR OF LIFE

Water Ambulance

If there is a fire on board a boat, or along a shoreline, then **fireboat** to the rescue!

Fireboats have powerful hoses that pump water directly from the ocean, lake or river.

They can spray water as high up as a skyscraper (400 feet or 122 metres)!

Fireboat

Patrol boats **watch over and protect waterbodies, like bays and harbours close to cities. They make sure people are following water traffic laws, and they fight crime on ships and shorelines. They may also help with border patrol and environmental protection.**

Many police boats have hoses and can help fight fires. Many of the police officers who work on police boats also know about firefighting, first aid and water safety.

Patrol Boat

Some patrol boats have crew that are city police officers, and some have crew that belong to the coast guard.

UNION COUNTY

POLICE

HOMELAND SECURITY

If people get into trouble on the water, search and rescue boats find them and help them.

Search and Rescue Boat

The US Coast Guard's lifeboat can weather hurricane force winds. It can also turn right-side up in 10 seconds if it flips over in the water. First aid supplies are kept in a waterproof area in the centre of the ship.

Search and rescue boats can tow other boats. For example, if a boat's engine stops working, then the rescue boat can pull it to safety.

When the ocean is covered in ice, but a ship has to get through to get supplies to Arctic workers, icebreaker ship to the rescue!

Some icebreaker ships have a specially curved bow at the front of the boat that allows the boat to slide on top of the ice. The weight of the boat breaks the ice as the boat moves forward.

Icebreaker Ship

If the ice is extra thick (taller than a person) the ship may ram the ice under full power to break it. One icebreaker ship broke through ice 40 feet (12 metres) thick. That is taller than a city bus is long!

The part of a boat that touches the water is called the hull. An icebreaker ship often has two hulls with only a small space between them. If the outside hull is damaged by ice, the inner hull protects the ship from taking on water.

What is an **amphibious truck**? It is a truck that is also a boat!

Some amphibious trucks spin their wheels to move forward in the water.

Amphibious Truck

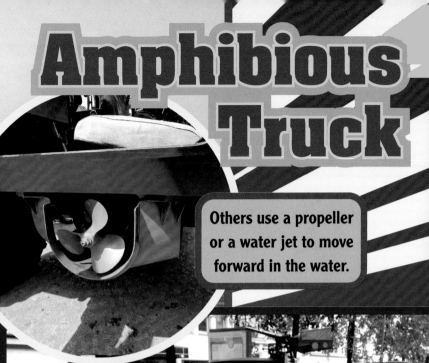

Others use a propeller or a water jet to move forward in the water.

I LIFTS
ATION
L CLEAR

Amphibious trucks move faster on land than they do in the water. They help out when there are floods or when army trucks need to be able to cross rivers or swamps.

A hovercraft can move easily between water and land.

It glides on a cushion of air made by a lot of fans.

Rescue Hovercraft

Hovercrafts are used for rescue missions because they travel easily on water, sand, swampland, snow and ice.

The Canadian Coast Guard and the U.S. Marine Corps use hovercrafts.

Hovercraft

Some large hovercrafts are fitted with an onboard crane that can lift up to 14,550 pounds (6600 kg). That is more than the average car weighs.

For big emergencies, rescue vehicles often work together.

Working Together

Rescue teams can include trucks, cars, vans, planes, helicopters, hovercraft and boats!

New kinds of rescue vehicles are always being built. Scientists are working on making solar-powered water ambulances. They use solar panels instead of fuel.

Do you have any ideas for cool rescue vehicles?

The Publisher: Mega Machines is an imprint of Blue Bike Books

Library and Archives Canada Cataloguing in Publication

Title: To the rescue! : emergency vehicles / Genevieve Boyer & Super Explorers.
Other titles: Emergency vehicles
Names: Boyer, Genevieve, author. | Super Explorers (Organization), author.
Identifiers: Canadiana (print) 20220402833 | Canadiana (ebook) 20220402965 | ISBN 9781989209400 (softcover) | ISBN 9781989209417 (PDF)
Subjects: LCSH: Emergency vehicles—Juvenile literature.
Classification: LCC TL235.8 .B69 2023 | DDC j629.225—dc23

Project Director: Peter Boer
Design & Layout: Ryschell Dragunov

Front cover credits: GettyImages: aragami123345/Thinkstock; super heroes, julos/Thinkstock.

Back cover credits: GettyImages: PA2 Zac Crawford, Graeme Main, nightman1965

Photo Credits: Every effort has been made to accurately credit the sources of photographs and illustrations. Any errors or omissions should be reported directly to the publisher for correction in future editions.

From Flickr: 7th Army Training Command, 54; Alan Paterson, 62; AR Military Sealift Command, 71; AR US Department of Agriculture, 49; AR USAG- Humphreys, 57; AR USArmy, 59; AR-USAG Humphreys, 37; Army Southern European Task Force, 54; Conal, 12; Frank Pierson, 23; Ian Press, 13; IPlayHockey, 67; Jason Lawrence, 27; Jason Lawrence, 27; Mitchell Smith, 22; Paul Townley, 13; Presidio of Monterey, 23; Presidio of Monteroy, 28; The National Guard, 55; Tony Hisgett, 66; Tyler Silvest, 17; From

From GettyImages: aapsky, 6; Ali Çobanoğlu, 7; andriano_cz, 21; Anton Minin, 20; Bazza1960,72; BERKO85, 5; Bulent-BARIS, 10; CRobertson, 16; digital94086, 18; Dmitry Karyshev, 3; Dmitry Karyshev, 44; DoroO, 34; Dushlik, 21; edb3_16, 46; egdigital, 79; Elijah-Lovkoff, 15; EvrenKalinbacak, 32, 33; Far700, 36; ffaber53, 48; Grigorenko, 45; huettenhoelscher, 38; IPGGutenbergUKLtd, 4; ivansmuk, 52; ivansmuk, 53; acquesdurocher, 19; JaGné, 16; Jochen Sand, 11; Jupiterimages, 9; kandypix, 28; Kenn Sharp, 39; kingjon 3, 14; liveslow, 5; LYagovy, 70; Maksim Safaniuk, 7; MariusLtu, 51; MattGush, 8; MJ_Prototype, 11; monkeybusinessimages, 8; nightman1965, 64; Pavel Byrkin, 19; poco, 15; RanieriMeloni, 65; Rockfinder, 36; Ryan McVay, 44; sangbog choi, 50; Sonate, 35; Stockbyte, 17; Stocktrek Images, 56; strevens, 74; Surf-Skate-Ski, 47; taburton, 49; Terry Seward,73; egdigital, 79; thehague, 78; Thinkstock Images, 53; Thinkstock, 52; Vagengeym_Elena, 20;

From Wikimedia: Alaska Air National Guard,43; AlfvanBeem, 73; AlfvanBeem, 73; AR Alaska and California National Guard,42; Cpl. James P. Aguilar US Marine Corps, 58; Department of Defense Current Photos, 69; Gerald Nino, 61; Gopal Aggarwal, 39; Graeme Main, 24, 25; Jamelle Bouie, 30; Jason Blackeye, 61; Jastrow, 73; Jeff Viano, USN, 72; Michael L Baird, 68; OGL Andrew Linnett, 40; Pamela Boehland, 69; ru_user_VMM, 77; Terry Seward, 40; UK Department for International Development, 60; Zac Crawford 76;

Superhero Illustrations: julos/Thinkstock.

Produced with the assistance of the Government of Alberta, Alberta Media Fund.   *Alberta*

We acknowledge the financial support of the Government of Canada through the Canada Book Fund for our publishing activities.

Funded by the Government of Canada   Financé par le gouvernement du Canada | **Canadä**

Printed in China

PC: 38-1